Capitalization and Punctuation

Kara Murray

PowerKiDS press™

New York

Published in 2014 by The Rosen Publishing Group, Inc.
29 East 21st Street, New York, NY 10010

First Edition

Editor: Amelie von Zumbusch
Book Design: Colleen Bialecki

Photo Credits: Cover Elyse Lewin/The Image Bank/Getty Images; p. 5 Hill Street Studios/Matthew Palmer/ Blend Images/Getty Images; p. 7 wavebreakmedia/Shutterstock.com; p. 8 Lisa F. Young/Shutterstock.com; p. 9 Jupiterimages/Pixland/Thinkstock; p. 11 Monkey Business Images/Shutterstock.com; p. 12 Frank Herholdt/The Image Bank/Getty Images; p. 13 George Doyle/Stockbyte/Getty Images; p. 15 Darrin Klimek/Lifesize/Getty Images; p. 16 tukkata/Shutterstock.com; p. 17 Comstock/Thinkstock; p. 18 kurhan/Shutterstock.com; p. 19 AISPIX by Imagesource/Shutterstock.com; p. 21 Hung Chung Chih/ Shutterstock.com.

Library of Congress Cataloging-in-Publication Data

Murray, Kara.
 Capitalization and punctuation / By Kara Murray. — First Edition.
    pages cm. — (Core Language Skills)
 Includes index.
 ISBN 978-1-4777-0803-3 (library binding) — ISBN 978-1-4777-0980-1 (pbk.) —
 ISBN 978-1-4777-0981-8 (6-pack)
 1. English language—Punctuation—Juvenile literature. 2. English language—Capitalization—Juvenile literature. I. Title.
 PE1450.M87 2014
 428.2'3—dc23

                                             2012049464

Manufactured in the United States of America

CPSIA Compliance Information: Batch #S13PK5: For Further Information contact Rosen Publishing, New York, New York at 1-800-237-9932

Contents

Capitalization and Punctuation

Capitalization is writing the first letter of a word as a capital letter. As you likely know, capital letters are larger than lowercase letters and have different shapes. "A" is a capital letter, while "a" is lowercase. Capitalization has many uses, but mainly it tells us when we are starting a new sentence and when we are coming across a special word in a sentence.

Chart of Common Punctuation

Name	Symbol	Example
Apostrophe	'	Tyler's house
Comma	,	Justin, Josh, and Emily
Exclamation point	!	I won!
Question mark	?	What time is it?
Period	.	I have two brothers.

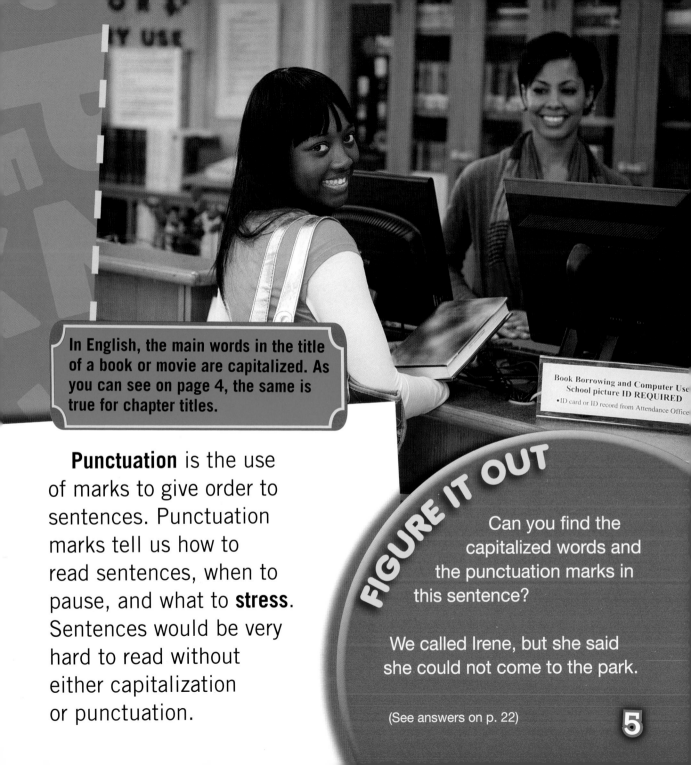

In English, the main words in the title of a book or movie are capitalized. As you can see on page 4, the same is true for chapter titles.

Punctuation is the use of marks to give order to sentences. Punctuation marks tell us how to read sentences, when to pause, and what to **stress**. Sentences would be very hard to read without either capitalization or punctuation.

Book Borrowing and Computer Use School picture ID REQUIRED
• ID card or ID record from Attendance Office

FIGURE IT OUT

Can you find the capitalized words and the punctuation marks in this sentence?

We called Irene, but she said she could not come to the park.

(See answers on p. 22)

The First Capital

One use for capital letters is to start sentences. The first letter of a new sentence is always capitalized. This signals to the reader to pause a bit when reading because a new thought is coming.

Have you ever written a letter to a friend or family member? We follow certain rules when writing letters. For example, you should start a letter with a **salutation**. A common salutation is "Dear." Salutations are always capitalized. You end a letter with special words, too. A common way to sign a letter is with "Sincerely." The words used to sign letters are always capitalized, too.

Writing a letter to a relative, such as your grandmother, is a great way to practice using capitalization.

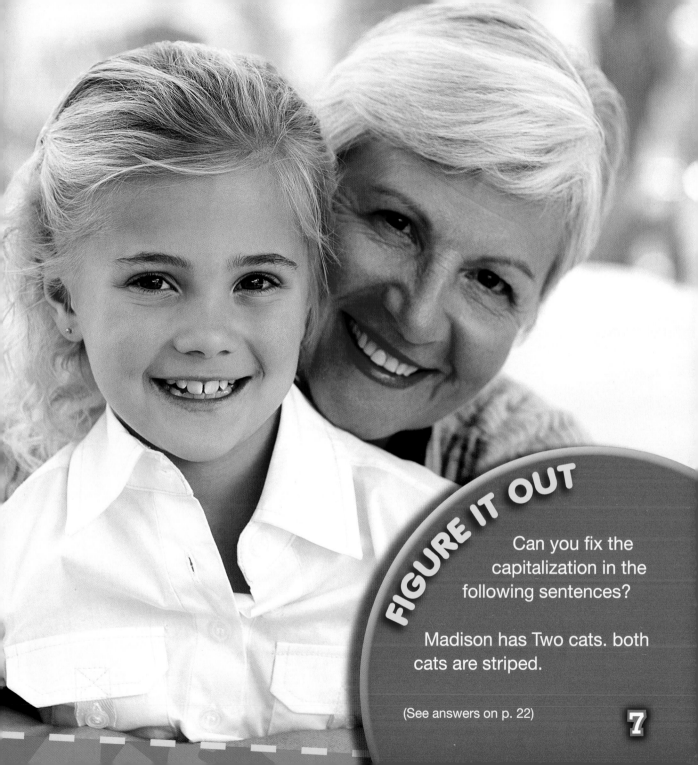

FIGURE IT OUT

Can you fix the capitalization in the following sentences?

Madison has Two cats. both cats are striped.

(See answers on p. 22)

Names

The first thing you learned to write was likely your name. Names always start with capital letters. In fact, all proper nouns start with capitals. **Proper nouns** are the names of specific places, people, and things. "Lassie" is a proper noun, but "dog" is an ordinary **noun**.

"Dad" is a proper noun in "I beat Dad!" It is not one in "My dad likes video games." That is because "dad" is used as a name in the first sentence only.

Many of the items you buy in a grocery store have brand names, such as Doritos or Rice Krispies. Can you come up with three other examples?

Product and brand names are also capitalized. For example, Cheerios might be your favorite breakfast cereal and Legos your favorite toys. Some, but not all, places have specific names. Your house likely doesn't have a name, but the street that it is on probably does. Street names are always capitalized.

FIGURE IT OUT

Is the capitalization correct in the following sentence?

At Rachel's house, we played my favorite games, monopoly and clue.

(See answers on p. 22)

Dates and Days

Days of the week, such as Friday and Tuesday, should always be capitalized. When you write a date, make sure to capitalize the name of the month. An example of this would be in the sentence, "Tomorrow is May 17." Seasons, such as spring or winter, are not usually capitalized.

What are your favorite days of the year? Is one of them a holiday? Holidays are special days. Some holidays are religious, like Christmas, Easter, and Hanukkah. Some are national holidays, like Thanksgiving and Independence Day. Capitalize the names of all holidays, no matter what kind they are.

Halloween is on October 31. The words "Halloween" and "October" are both always capitalized.

FIGURE IT OUT

Is the capitalization correct in the following words?

February, father's day, sunday, Birthday, Monday

(See answers on p. 22)

11

Ending Marks

Sentences are ways of stating thoughts. They come in several types. Each type requires a particular kind of end punctuation, or punctuation that comes at the end of a sentence. For example, questions should end with question marks. Questions are things that are asked. One example is, "Where are you?"

Statements are the most common type of sentence. They express complete thoughts. Statements require periods at the end. Commands also usually end with periods.

The answer to a question is usually a statement. Let's say someone asked you, "What is the weather?" You might reply, "It is raining."

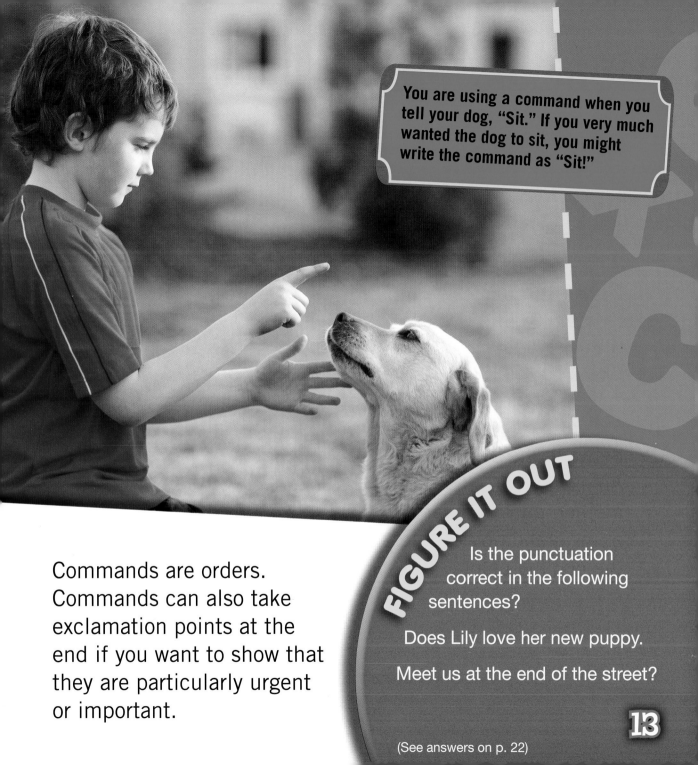

You are using a command when you tell your dog, "Sit." If you very much wanted the dog to sit, you might write the command as "Sit!"

Commands are orders. Commands can also take exclamation points at the end if you want to show that they are particularly urgent or important.

FIGURE IT OUT

Is the punctuation correct in the following sentences?

Does Lily love her new puppy.

Meet us at the end of the street?

13

(See answers on p. 22)

Commas in a Series

Commas are used for several purposes. They are one of the trickiest kinds of punctuation to master. In fact, people do not all use them the same way.

People use at least one comma when listing three or more things in a **series**. The last two things in a series are separated by the word "and." Commas separate any earlier words in the series. Some people also add a comma between the second-to-last word and "and." An example of this is the sentence, "My mother, my father, and my brother will all be at my grandmother's house." Others leave out the comma before "and."

If you forgot the first comma in "Mary, Ann, Chris, and Noah," people would think you were listing a girl named "Mary Ann" instead of a girl named "Mary" and a girl named "Ann."

FIGURE IT OUT

Are there any commas missing in the following sentence?

Ben Susan, and George are starting a hiking club.

(See answers on p. 22)

15

Commas in Dates and Letters

Another way commas are used is in dates. Dates are written in a specific order. In the United States, we write the month first, then the day of the month followed by a comma, and then the year followed by another comma. If the year is the last word in the sentence, a period is used after it instead of a comma.

If this calendar showed the month of July 2015, you would write the outlined date as July 29, 2015.

You might sign a letter to a family member or someone else who means a lot to you with the word "Love." A comma should separate "Love" and your name.

Commas also have special uses in letters. After the salutation, you write the name of the person to whom you are writing. A comma follows the name. The word you use to sign your letter, such as "Sincerely," should also be followed by a comma.

FIGURE IT OUT

Is the use of commas correct in the following sentence?

On December, 7 2012 my little sister was born.

(See answers on p. 22)

Apostrophes with Contractions

Apostrophes have several uses. Let's discuss apostrophes in **contractions**. A contraction is a shortened form of two words. In it, an apostrophe takes the place of the missing letter or letters. Some common contractions are combinations of **pronouns** and **verbs**. For example, the contraction "he's" is short for "he is." "You've" is short for "you have," and "I'll" is short for "I will."

The Reeds just bought their new house. They haven't moved in yet. The contraction "haven't" is short for "have not."

Another commonly used type of contraction is the negative form of a verb. Some of these contractions include "don't," short for "do not," "can't," short for "cannot," and "isn't," short for "is not."

There are two contractions in the sentence, "I'm glad we're friends." "I'm" is short for "I am," and "we're" is short for "we are."

FIGURE IT OUT

How could you rewrite this sentence using contractions?

I could not believe that he did not want to come.

(See answers on p. 22)

Possessives

Apostrophes are also used with possessives. **Possessives** show that certain nouns possess, or have, things. "Nathan's" is possessive in the sentence, "I like Nathan's dog." You add an apostrophe and an "s" to form the possessive with **singular** nouns. You do the same with **plural** nouns that do not end in "s." For plural nouns that end in "s," add an apostrophe to the end of the word. An example is "the boys' mother."

Punctuation and capitalization make reading easier. When you learn the rules for both and use them correctly, your readers will have an easier time understanding the things that you write.

The plural possessive form of the word "panda" is "pandas'." You might use it in the sentence, "The pandas' fur looks so soft."

FIGURE IT OUT

How would you form possessives for the following nouns?

Tim, violin, messages, geese

(See answers on p. 22)

21

Figure It Out: The Answers

Page 5: The capital letters are the "W" in "We" and the "I" in "Irene." The punctuation marks used are the comma after "Irene" and the period at the end of the sentence.

Page 7: "Two" should not be capitalized in the first sentence. In the second sentence, "both" should be capitalized.

Page 9: "Monopoly" and "Clue" should both be capitalized since they are brand names for games and, therefore, proper nouns.

Page 11: "Father's Day" should be capitalized, as should "Sunday." "Birthday" should not be capitalized unless it begins a sentence.

Page 13: No, it is not. The first sentence is a question and should have a question mark at the end. The second sentence is a command and should have a period at the end.

Page 15: There is a comma missing after "Ben." The sentence should read, "Ben, Susan, and George are starting a hiking club."

Page 17: No, it is not. The sentence should read, "On December 7, 2012, my little sister was born."

Page 19: You would rewrite the sentence: "I couldn't believe that he didn't want to come."

Page 21: The correct possessives are: Tim's, violin's, messages', geese's.

Glossary

capitalization (ka-pih-tuh-lih-ZAY-shun) Starting words with a capital, or uppercase, letter.

contractions (kon-TRAK-shunz) Shortened forms of a word or words that use apostrophes in the place of missing letters.

noun (NOWN) A person, place, idea, state, or thing.

plural (PLUR-el) Having to do with more than one.

possessives (puh-ZEH-sivz) Words that show having or ownership.

pronouns (PRO-nowns) Words that can take the place of nouns.

proper nouns (PRAH-per NOWNZ) Nouns that name particular people, places, or things.

punctuation (punk-choo-WAY-shun) The use of periods, commas, and other marks to help make the meaning of a sentence clear.

salutation (sal-yuh-TAY-shun) A word or words of greeting that come at the beginning of a letter.

series (SEER-eez) A group of similar things that come one after another.

singular (SING-gyuh-lur) Having to do with just one.

stress (STREHS) The extra force put in a part of a word when it is spoken.

verbs (VERBZ) Words that describe actions.

Index

Websites

Due to the changing nature of Internet links, PowerKids Press has developed an online list of websites related to the subject of this book. This site is updated regularly. Please use this link to access the list:

www.powerkidslinks.com/cls/cap/